Perfection

What if everything were perfect...

Written By
Vito R. DeLuca Jr.

Copyright © 2007 by Vito R. DeLuca Jr.

All rights reserved. No part of this book may be reproduced or transmitted in any form or by any means, electronic or mechanical, including photocopying, recording, or by any information storage and retrieval system, without permission in writing from the Author.

ISBN: 978-0-6151-5554-8

Copyrighted Material

Perfection perfects through imperfection...

Dedication:

To those who seek to understand life's trials and tribulations...

Introduction

The message in this book came to me during a period of fasting and meditation. Throughout this 21-day period I kept getting the impulse to write down my thoughts. From these writings I've created several books. I believe this book delivers one of the most powerful messages.

It may be difficult to accept at first—especially if you do not read through to the end—but I promise if you will read the entire message you will discover the beauty in what may seem on the surface to be imperfect.

Read this message with an open mind and allow the possibility that it just may change your view on life.

What if everything were perfect?

I don't mean what if everything were perfect as you imagine perfect to be.

In other words, I don't mean what if you had everything you ever wanted: the perfect relationship, the perfect house, the perfect children, or the perfect job as you imagine them to be.

What I mean is; What if everything in your life as it is right now was perfectly as it should be?

What if your relationships were—by design—the way they are to help you to learn and grow?

What if your children were the way they are to test you and give you a chance to prove your character?

What if everything in your life (right now) is perfectly there to help you become perfected?

You might ask, "What about the newborns who come into this world imperfect?" What about them? What did they do wrong to be burdened with their imperfection?

What about the young child who gets cancer? Is that perfect? What did she do to deserve that?

I could argue that the parents may need some character building but it would still beg the question, "Why does the poor child have to be burdened?"

What if a child is born imperfect or contracts a life-threatening disease? Is it possible that this child is a gift to their parents or maybe the world?

Is it possible that the imperfection or disease is a gift to the child?

Is it possible that the parents are in need of a certain stress in their lives—to wake them up out of their selfish lives—to help them perfect themselves?

Please bear with me on this. I'm sure on the surface this is hard to accept.

I promise you will understand where I'm coming from by the time you've finished reading.

Maybe this child is here to teach others and help others to see the imperfection in themselves.

Maybe the child was born for a reason—a perfect reason.

Most often when you speak to people who have had a hard life, who have dealt with a sick child, or who have been through some terrible tragedy in their lives, you will hear a story of triumph, a story of overcoming the odds, or a story of people perfecting their souls through this tragic experience.

And you will also often hear them say they wouldn't change it for the world.

Have you ever heard the story of Helen Keller?

If you haven't you should take the time to read about her. Better yet, rent the movie *The Miracle Worker.*

Do you think Helen Keller would have changed anything?

Do you think that, if she had the opportunity to do it all over, she would have chosen to come back a perfectly healthy and normal child?

Would anyone who has learned great lessons from her life think that the world would have been better served if Helen Keller never existed as she did?

She was truly a gift to this world and she wouldn't have changed a thing.

Could you be living the perfect life right now and just not know it?

What do you need to learn?

What is happening in your life right now that seems imperfect but may just be perfectly there to give you an opportunity to learn?

Could there possibly be a perfect reason for everything going on in your life right now?

Could there possibly be a perfect reason for everything going on in the world?

Could there possibly be a perfect reason for everything going on in the universe?

This was just a thought I had while pondering life.

But as my wife always likes to remind me, it's just one man's opinion.

Actually it was just a thought that I started to ponder.

What do you think?

"Although the world is full of suffering, it is full also of the overcoming of it."

Helen Keller

"We could never learn to be brave and patient, if there were only joy in the world."

Helen Keller

"Life is either a daring adventure or nothing. Security does not exist in nature, nor do the children of men as a whole experience it. Avoiding danger is no safer in the long run than exposure."

Helen Keller

Perfection

What if this world were perfect
Just as perfect as can be

As it is right now
With no exchange for what you see

Would you be upset
That God would leave us in this mess

And call what we see *perfect*
All this pain and hell and stress

Or would you see perfection
In a lonely child's cry

Or in a breast with cancer
Or a war that's gone awry

The mystery of God's great plan
Is full of love and pain

And unknown to us mortal souls
Upon this earthly plain

But what if you could see the *why*
Of what you see as wrong

To understand the message
In a sickly child's song

The day will come when all's revealed
To each and every one

That this strange world was perfect
And then all will be undone

For all the things that you will judge
As ugly to your tastes

Will be revealed as lessons to a world
Where there's no waste

The sickly kid and cancered breast
Are gifts from up above

And war is *too* a message
In this perfect world of love

These things are right but you won't see
Until you drop your view

To judge the world's perfection
Is to think as if you knew

But you can't see a perfect world
Because you have a need

A need to judge the judger
A need you must concede

But what if you would let the grace
Reveal within your heart

The cry of lonely children
May just be the place to start

To start to see that this small space
That spans through all of time

Is where you learn the lessons
Of your life's eternal rhyme

For when you see that life's a blink
That we spend on this earth

You'll see the world's perfection
And that all that's bad has worth

Yes when we pass beyond this place
To endless space and time

You'll know that life upon this earth
Was perfect and sublime

For while you're here the things you see
Are messages to you

To learn the things you need to learn
Before your time is through

So look beyond the pain you see
And what may be revealed

Are lessons sent for you to learn
It's *you* who needs to heal

The sickly child that needs your love
Was sent for you to see

Your selfish ways must be removed
Before you can be free

The cancered breast reveals a pain
Resentment brought to bear

To see this will release the cells
That heal the shell you wear

And what of war played out by men
Who miss the greater point

What does this teach to all of us
To whom does this anoint

I tell you now I can't explain
The details of it all

But I can see beyond it
To the place before the fall

For once you see the pattern in
The pain you see in life

You recognize perfection
In this pain that seems so rife

I'll leave you now with just one thought
That just may help you see

That sickness and the wars at hand
Are part of heavens key

Now do you know the story of
A girl named Helen Keller

Who started out as broken
But whose life became quite stellar

And do you think that it was wrong
For her to start out bad

With nothing to be thankful for
Or no way to be glad

Well if you do I might just ask

What makes you think you're right

To judge this girl's perfection

Is to see without the light

So ponder that as you move through

This flicker in space time

And you may see perfection in

This intricate design

The more you stop and wait to see

Beyond this one dimension

The more you'll see that what's revealed

Is nothing but perfection

"Character cannot be developed in ease and quiet. Only through experience of trial and suffering can the soul be strengthened, ambition inspired, and success achieved."

Helen Keller

The Beginning...

"The world is perfect because good cannot exist without evil. In other words, there would be no physical world at all if evil did not exist."

Vito R. DeLuca Jr.

www.ingramcontent.com/pod-product-compliance
Lightning Source LLC
Chambersburg PA
CBHW051718040426
42446CB00008B/939